Sez She

A Play

by Jane Martin

A SAMUEL FRENCH ACTING EDITION

SAMUEL FRENCH

FOUNDED 1830

New York   Hollywood   London   Toronto

SAMUELFRENCH.COM

ISBN   978-0-573-63343-0   Printed   in   U.S.A.   #20890

IMPORTANT BILLING AND CREDIT REQUIREMENTS

All producers of **SEZ SHE** must give credit to the Author of the Play in all programs distributed in connection with performances of the Play, and in all instances in which the title of the Play appears for the purposes of advertising, publicizing or otherwise exploiting the Play and /or a production. The name of the Author must appear on a separate line on which no other name appears, immediately following the title and must appear in size of type not less than fifty percent of the size of the title type.

AUTHOR'S NOTE

SEZ SHE is a monologue play written to be performed by five actresses. Each actress would perform either seven or eight monologues, which basically equates with a leading role for each. The author does not suggest how the monologues should be assigned but leaves that to the discretion of the director. You will find an order listed here and some rudimentary suggestions for staging, but both may be disregarded to suit the talents involved. An appendix appears at the end of the text with five additional pieces that may be substituted for those the author has selected. From experience with an earlier monologue play, VITAL SIGNS*, the number of twenty pieces per act should not be exceeded, but each act could contain as few as eighteen. SEZ SHE has been written with a simple scheme in mind. This is a play you could do on a bare stage with a few chairs and a table or, if wished, something more elaborate. There are a couple of specific costumes notes, as necessary, and the actresses should be scheduled in a way that allows for these changes. In the main, it is imagined that the actresses would wear one contemporary outfit throughout except for the few specific changes mentioned. A sound score would be good. Have fun.

*There should be one 10-15 minute intermission.

ACT I

Kindness
Duke
Corporate Views
On the Wing
Luther
Wet Grass
Mom
Dazzle
Nap
Kandahar Road
Suntan
True Love
Breath
Spray
Class War
Twinkies
Beans
Fly Me to the Moon
Sex

ACT II

APPENDIX

ACT I

(An empty stage, a single actress. Gradually, during the piece, four other actresses drift onto the stage and listen.)

KINDNESS

ACTRESS. You know what I think has gotten devalued in the 21st century? Kindness. It's sort of gotten to be a second-rate virtue. You know how people who don't think you're pretty will always tell you you have nice hair? How they say what a 'kind' person you are and then they never call back for a second date. So I started asking people if anything nice had happened to them this week and everything they mentioned was a form of kindness, you know, somebody picking up something they dropped or walking them to a place they were trying to find or taking the trouble to return a lost item or incorrectly addressed piece of mail, and I thought, everybody loves it, they've just forgotten its name. So I started applauding. Whenever I would see a kindness done I would start applauding and when people asked why I would tell them, and this guy I applauded had a drive-time radio show and he put me on and the next day I saw someone else applaud and then someone else and then there was a bumper sticker, "Applaud Kindness," and about a month later this older man applauded and then everyone else on the street did too and this guy who had stopped his car so this lady could push a stroller across got

SEZ SHE

out of the car and bowed. It was fantastic. So anyway I don't know why I brought this up, it's old news by now... but it was really nice of you to listen all the way through.

(She applauds. The other actresses join in and, as they applaud, three of them and the speaker sit around the stage. The narrative is picked up by the actress left standing.)

DUKE

ACTRESS. Duke? Here boy. Dinner-time, Duke. Mama, have you seen Duke? That dog has been so erratic since the divorce. He won't eat a thing but table scraps and every night he lies on Austin's side of the bed whining until I have to put him out. Duke? Oh my God, Mama, get in here. Hurry. Oh my God, you won't believe this. Look. Look out there. Duke has jumped off the garage deck and impaled himself on the picket fence. No, don't go out there, he's obviously gone. It's a nightmare. Poor Duke. How on earth did he climb up there, Mama? The Pekinese is not a climber. He must have gone upstairs, gotten out on the second floor balcony, walked along that little ledge, made a leap for the garage, which is an incredible feat for a dog of that size, and then once on the garage deck gotten a running start, gone at top speed and flung himself out to get to that picket fence. Mama, Duke has committed suicide, there is no other explanation. He is a canine victim of this catastrophic divorce. He should have gone with Austin, Mama, I should have insisted. Our children are traumatized, Austin's lost his job because he worked for Daddy, the grass died because I forgot to water, the car's been repossessed and now it's all topped off with an impaled Pekinese. Oh no, the neighbors are gathering, I just can't take any more of this. They say that in every relationship one of the partners invariably loves more, and I see now it's undoubtedly Duke. Mama, bring me the cordless phone because I am going to have to call that hateful man and do my best to reconcile with him before the house spontaneously combusts or we all contract mad cow disease. I know a sign or portent when I see one, Mama, and a Pekinese with a stake through its heart is just about as clear as it gets. *(One of the cast hands her a cell phone.)* Austin, it's Alma, I believe we have to talk.

(She moves to the side of the stage talking quietly on the cell phone as another actress rises who is wearing a beach robe. During "Corporate Views," she takes off the robe, revealing her swimsuit, and applies sun lotion.)

CORPORATE VIEWS

ACTRESS. "Paul Ringo," I would say, 'cause he was named after half of you-know-who... "Paul Ringo, we have got to take our destiny into our own hands. We are nuthin' but wage slaves bein' hung out to dry by corporate malfeasance. We got to get in on the malfeasance end. We need the capital in capitalism, baby, to get us off the bottom rung of the ladder." Paul Ringo, he says, "Buttercup,"... which isn't a given name but a term of endearment, "Buttercup, I am headed to the loan desk of the Bank of America and when I come back we are getting into sundries." He said he saw sundries in our future. Well, Paul Ringo, his word is his bond and, as of July 1, we was running Lundy's Sundries in Crestfall, West Virginia, with one and a half employees, open a half-day Sunday. Now, come September we was vergin' on the net positive... hey, nose drops and chewin' tobacco were goin' through the roof when the devil's scourge showed up at Exit 42. Oh yeah. Lemme tell you one thing here, Wal-Mart opens down the road, you can kiss your sundries goodbye. Bam! In a microsecond we was lucky to do ten dollars a day and I said, "Paul Ringo, we got to free our inner-entrepreneur!" Now Lundy's Sundries was occupyin' a former firehouse with the brass pole extant, an' I studied on that brass pole an' I achieved illumination. I yelled out "Paul Ringo, welcome to resurrection." See, back a few years, I was a moderately exotic dancer name of "the Pocket Rocket," and a pole like that, it had personal resonance. From that day forth at five to the hour on the hour the "the Pocket Rocket" slithered down that pole and into the chips, dips and cereals section, and I gave those wide-eyed customers five big minutes of hell on wheels. Crowds? Uh-huh. We kind of cornered the market on your middle-aged male shopper. Bought them one hell of a lot of Triple A batteries. Wasn't three months before the Wal-Mart Satan bought us out for three quarters of a million dollars. You write that down in Das Kapitol! Paul Ringo an' me we're semi-permanent now on the southeast side of the Isle of Tabago, drinkin' fruit concoctions with a high alcohol content. I let Crestfall, West Virginia get a good look at my sundries and I brought Wal-Mart to its knees. Put that in your M.B.A. and smoke it.

(She lies down on a beach towel and "suns" herself during the next speech. Someone places a chair for the actress doing "On the Wing.")

ON THE WING

ACTRESS. James, you have to... you need to calm down... you do, you need to look at me. We can't... put this off... anymore, Jimmy. We just can't because... well, we both know why. We never say why, but we know, and we go to bed with it and we wake up with it and it's in us when we play with the kids or take them for an overnight. Thank you for looking at me. Thank you. He said today it's going to come fast now. He said it would probably be over by the end of the summer. Actually he said he was... sure. There. I'm so sorry. I'm so sorry, my darling. But it's good to know in a way, right? I'm glad to know, I really am. I'm amazed, but I am. Keep looking at me, okay? You can't handle the kids, James, and do the work you do. A nanny, yes. In the very short term, yes, but... James, this is going to be the hard part, but it will only last a minute and the very strange thing is it turns out to be a good thing... all things being situational, right? Now I want you to let me say this and not say anything back. When I stop, then you can talk but, really, you don't need to. First of all, I love you and I'll keep loving you. That is... unchangeable. Truly. Now this next part will...go better...if I do it in a rush, it just will. You've been having an affair for two years with Laura, starting about a year after I got sick, which I've known for fourteen months and she's known I know for six months which made her want to stop, but I convinced her not to and, as you know, she hasn't. Now that's out. That's better. Jimmy, I admire the way she raises her child single-handed and her house shines and her car's waxed and she works at home and she has such nice shoes, and we talk quite a bit now and it's clear she loves you and obviously, from all you do for her, you care for her and she likes the kids so you have to admit it would be a perfect situation...afterwards...it would be. Please don't look so stricken. It's all right, really it is. What time is it, darling? You know I told her that I was going to tell you this afternoon and I think...well, I know...that it would be generous if you drove over to see Laura before her son comes home from school and told her not to worry, that we talked and it was fine. We are fine, aren't we? Just for an hour, James, she'll be worried. Go now. Go. We can talk about it when you get home. We can talk about it until fall.

(She gets up and takes the chair off stage. The "sunbather" also EXITS. The two actresses bring on tall wooden stools. One is the speaker of "Luther," the other simply an acquaintance at the bar. One of the cast represents the bartender who is, in fact,

SEZ SHE

Luther.)

LUTHER

ACTRESS. Hey, Luther, set me up another beer, okay? Maybe two, lights, and a shot. What a day, okay? Jeez, a day in the life of Lorraine.Yeah, yeah, you know me as Jackie, but my innermost self, that's a Lorraine. Fat chance, right? Like I would suddenly wake up svelte with creamy skin and long natural lashes. Anyway, six a.m. I got a rat in my kitchen. And by the way a rat is not a mouse. Close to a foot long and hostile. And I think, Lorraine, remember you are a fortunate citizen of the greatest country in recorded history and into each life a little rat must fall. So, after some skirmishing, I simply leave on the basis that what gets in could also get out and I go to my car which, zingo, has been broken into. So, Luther... another shot... this leads me to the thought, "What, for the ordinary person...a Jackie Moskowitz sort of person, is happiness?" And I'm on the bus mulling this over when a guy stands up and starts to pee in the aisle. Yeah. And at that precise moment, Luther, I see what happiness is. Shove those peanuts down here. Not the pretzels, the peanuts. Happiness, Luther, is uninterrupted routine with no surprises. Pretty good, huh? So I share this thought with the guy on the bus who stops what he's doing and gives the idea due consideration. He thinks, he zips up, he says "What about nice surprises?" Okay, I'll consider this. I write down in my notebook, he counts on his fingers, we both come up with overwhelmingly negative surprises. He amends to say his house got chosen for a TV makeover show, but the designer had a thing for cornhusks. Look, people come in here to the bar, Luther, you say what's up, they say "same old, same old, same old" like this was a problem, a disappointment, whereas in point of fact that which we call boredom is actually exquisite happiness, but because happiness turns out to be boring you never recognize it. Never, that is, Luther, until the rat gets into the kitchen or the bus becomes a lavatory. You, for instance, Luther, silent as a stone, do nothing but the expected, serve nothing but the expected, and say nothing but the expected which is exactly why you got regulars. Set me up another beer, Luther. Where else would I want to be?

(The bar stools are removed. The stage empties except for the actress doing "Wet Grass.")

WET GRASS

ACTRESS. My life is very...plain. Unadorned. A ham sandwich sort of life. A nine to five, television, Sonicare, electric blanket, parents for Sunday dinner kind of life. Very...purchasable. It's not surprising and I'm not surprising...I'm never surprised not to be found surprising. A matte sort of life, no sheen. But I started taking walks, walks at night, seeing people through the windows, nine to five people doing the nondescript: folding laundry, working on scrapbooks, scrubbing pots, straightening pictures. It's quiet and cold and, through the glass, it seems an enactment of mysteries, rituals, and the people are serious and concentrated and skillful and it's like a kind of dancing. Sometimes they just stand still, lost in thought and I take them for interesting, sizable thoughts that, if they were written, would be poetry. I stand there on the grass with my slippers soaking through with dew and even the least of them are beautiful because they are...completely unselfconscious. A wonderful silent movie. I think you are beautiful. It's why I come to the carwash. I sit in the car and you soap and shine and sponge and chamois through the downpour, a mysterious, riveting mime. I live on the ground floor at 1806 Springwillow, and I wonder...I wonder if you might stand on my lawn tonight and watch me...watch my commonplaces, watch me vacuum or...because then perhaps you would think me mysterious and even...even beautiful. Because being seen in that way it could...it might permeate me, enter me, change me, knowing what you felt standing on the wet grass. And when I was that new thing, why then I would come here and meet you and tell you...tell you my commonplace name. Come tonight, before the Sonicare. Please come. I need to be seen.

(She stands for a second while another actress enters dressed in whatever eighth grade "popular" girls are wearing when Sez She is produced. Once the actress doing "Mom" has said "...going out of this house wearing that!," the actress who did "Wet Grass" EXITS.)

MOM

ACTRESS. Oh my God. Mom! You are not, I am completely serious, going out of this house wearing that! Bitch me out. Do you know what you look like? You are mega-embarrassing, okay? Mom! You are representing me at the P.T.A., I can't have everybody's 8th grade parents seeing you in hooker wear. Ohmygod. Do you know how old you are? You are an ancient, decrepit person, Mom. Sorreee, but you are. Spaghetti straps, and don't tell me that skirt passes the finger test. Mom! Wait a minute, wait one minute, open your mouth and hold it open. Ohmygod, gross! Ohmygod, is that a tongue piercing? Mother, menopause and tongue piercing are polar opposites, okay? Mom, there is a dress code, you can't walk into the P.T.A. direct from the whore wars. God, Mom, have a little respect, will you, you're a dentist. I mean where are we headed here I would like to ask. Are you going to be one of those sixty-year-olds who look like steel prunes showing endless leg with plucked eyebrows and breast augmentation? I warn you, Mom, if you set foot in the P.T.A. I will get Dad and Aunt Lucy and your therapist and Father O'Keefe, and we'll do an intervention in the parking lot. I mean hand over the tanning salon discount coupons. You know, I'm sorry but the difference between who you are and who you think you are is an unbelievable sag factor. Now go upstairs this minute and put on something with long sleeves and flats. You can go to the meeting but, after that, ohmygod, you are soooo grounded!

(As the piece finishes, she moves upstage and is joined upstage by three other cast members who form an overlapping listening group. The actress who does "Dazzle" lies downstage of this group and begins.)

DAZZLE

ACTRESS. I was lying on my old cotton blanket in my backyard in Vincennes, Indiana down by the Illinois border, and I was trying to see a constellation called "Serpent Holder," which is this vast star group resembling a voodoo doctor holding the pieces of a snake torn in two, when they came for me. I saw this pinpoint of searing light, enlarging, coming straight for me, and it echoed outward so I was in a blinding circle of this...dazzle, and a gelatinous, translucent figure formed, a little like a bird inside out and though it didn't speak it resonated inside my head as...as an invitation and I stood and it moved toward me in a series of stop-images, and I tried to look away but I had no muscular control and it enveloped me and the light tightened, drew in around me and I felt a pressure which seemed calming and warming and it separated me from my body which fell to the ground like an old skin and as I was elevated the light created a series of rotating spheres, one inside the other, alternating a clockwise, anti-clockwise rotation and I was drawn upward at tremendous speed and the heat increased and I could sense I was melting but the sensation was pleasurable, until I was some form of sentient liquid endlessly shifting, a repository of thought that moves through me like a river and much of the thought is music, or color, or texture made available to the seven senses but not limited by them, and it was possible to experience a thousand lives simultaneously and that the greatest absurdity was that I had been afraid of death.

(At the end of "Dazzle," the speaker remains lying down and is joined by three other actresses in attitudes of sleep. The speaker of "Nap" stands.)

NAP

ACTRESS. I don't know about you but I go to the theatre to get a little sleep. I know, you think I'm kidding. Listen here, I have three kids so you know there's no sleep to be had at home...babies crying, cats throwing up hairballs, dogs barking at moths and a husband who can only identify a sexual urge at the break of dawn. I have to seek out public events to get a little peace and quiet. Even that's become difficult. Until the late 50's you could sleep at the movies...that was pre-car chase. Squeal, roar, crash, fireball! Impossible. Symphony halls? They always throw in one piece of contemporary music scored for an outboard motor and two chain saws. Libraries? They think you're homeless. Museums? There's always a docent whispering in your ear. We are a universally sleep-deprived nation. We're irritable, socially aggressive, politically schizoid; we have got to get some sleep! I know you know what I'm talking about. Great sex is okay, but eight hours of uninterrupted sleep is unbelievably erotic. I'm sorry, I'm sorry, I'm a little edgy. Are my hands shaking? My eyes are red, right? I am telling you, the theatre is the only place left to sleep. The soporific sound of endless conversation, a kind of white noise, a sort of verbal sea sound. Lull-ing situations you've seen a thousand times...delicious boredom. They talk for a long time and then they get divorced or they die a lingering death or they decide to... I don't know...live lives of quiet desperation. If it's Chekhov, there are fabulous pauses, one right after the other. Or Iambic pentameter, God, that would put anybody to sleep. But here's the best part, nobody ever wakes you because a) it's socially embarrassing or b) they're asleep, too. One time, a thoughtful woman next to me put her coat over me during King Lear and sang this really quiet lullaby — it was so touching. Sure, it's a little expensive, but hey, you wake up to applause...if you're disoriented the ushers are really nice about helping you out of the theatre. Once they just turned out the lights and left me there until morning. You could try it now. Go ahead. The next piece is really quiet and kind of hypnotic. Don't be shy, really. I'll get the actors to hold it down. Shhhh. Rockabye.

(At the end of "Nap," three of the actresses hunker down around the stage listening. The speaker of "Kandahar Road" caries a swaddled baby and eventually sits in a rocking chair.)

KANDAHAR ROAD

ACTRESS. Kandahar Road. I had my baby on Kandahar Road. Dusty, rutted, potholed, bandit-ridden, glorious Kandahar Road. Time out of mind in Afghanistan, way down upon the Tarnak River, a long, long time ago. A long time before the Taliban, a long time before anything you'd know about. There were places where apples and pears grew wild along the highway. I remember we stopped near Moqor and there was an old man in a half dead Lazy-Boy with an oil drum full of pears, and they were gray from the truck dust but impossibly sweet. I've never forgotten the silky taste of the pears on Kandahar Road. It was 305 miles from Kandahar to Kabul, but it

18

SEZ SHE

could take you six days to drive it. There were potholes like meteor
craters and children with old Turkish bolt-action rifles and pock-
marked young guys selling water that actually boiled in the sun.
My husband, back in that time, was an aid worker, food distributor,
for the British Red Cross, and I lived in Cicero, Illinois with a step-
son and a Welch spaniel, and he would come home twice a year and
I was so lonely I just flustered him into letting me get pregnant. I
woke up one morning eight months along and I wanted, I needed, I
was desperate to see my husband, and I flew to Kabul but the woman
with one tooth in his office said he was gone to Kandahar. His Red
Cross mates had an ancient helicopter, antique, and I caught a ride
with them but he wasn't in Kandahar, he had taken a food convoy to
Ghanzi, which is pretty tribal but it had a 16-bed working hospital
so I hired a taxi for fifty dollars American and went to find him. It
was three days from Kandahar to Ghanzi and I was carsick, so carsick, and the driver, Akmed the very large indeed, spoke no English
and I could never get him to stop the car, and he would never look
directly at me, and at night he slept under the car and I tried nine
ways of laying down on the seat. When the contractions started, I
tried to wake him but he slept like the dead, and when I threw stones
at him he locked me out of the taxi and drove off with my money
and my suitcase. Kandahar Road. After...oh, I don't know how many
hours, there was a Mack-built truck driven by a one-legged
Turkamen, and he mercifully stopped and gathered wood and heated
water, and he bowed a bow and fanned out a blanket I could lie on in
a gully by the Kandahar Road and, after thirteen hours, I had a little
girl and he cut the cord with a piece of tin he heated in the fire. Then
the merciful Turkamen turned his truck around, and we drove into
Ghanzi and he took me to the hospital. The hospital on Kandahar
Road. *(A pause.)* It turned out my husband had flown to Cicero to
surprise me by being there for the birth of my baby. Aimee Elizabeth. Aimee Elizabeth, midwifed my the one-legged Turkamen in

the gully by the truck on the moonlit Kandahar Road.

(The three listening actresses EXIT as does the "Kandahar Road"
speaker. The actress who does "Suntan" ENTERS wearing a
large T-shirt over a bathing suit. She is eating a red Popsicle.)

SUNTAN

ACTRESS. So, I was down at the beach. New Jersey shore. I had
my new suit on, which turned out to be too big, and I was burying
my cousin Carolina in the sand up to her neck, which, don't tell her
but I thought was a definite improvement, and I had the hole goin'
and I reached in and there was a bottle with a cork in it an' a note
inside, and we broke the bottle to get to it an' the note said "For
God's sake, take my last two wishes," you know like a joke. An'
Carolina, she said hell if she had a wish she'd want a cheeseburger
and a coke 'cause she was hungry as hell, either that or peace on
earth, but right now she'd prefer the burger an' we laughed, but
when we turned around there was a burger and a coke on her beach
towel. Okay, so that kind of turned our heads around backwards, if
you know what I mean? Sure, it had to be a joke but how did it
work? There was, I'm not kiddin', nobody within fifty yards of us.
Carolina and me broke out in a sweat. She starts to tear up and she
says to me, "I just wasted one of our two wishes on a cheeseburger?" "Yeah," I says, "an' you could have had peace on earth." So
we looked over at the burger, and a cockroach comes out from under the bun. Now that made us think, kinda tainted the burger, an' I
say, "Carolina, how come whoever had these wishes gave them
away?" We both agreed that was suspicious. So we're mulling that
over when a stick sits up and writes all by itself in the sand, "You
have three minutes left," and then it just keeled over and lay there
like a regular stick. So the seconds are tickin' away, and we realize

SEZ SHE

we're working with this time limit on a supernatural tainted wish down on the New Jersey shore. Scary, right? See, you are probably smart enough to figure out a good wish in a situation like that, but we couldn't come up with a damn thing 'til Carolina thought of her ex-boyfriend who stole her stereo and ran off to shack up with her best friend in Costa Rica, and that was three days before their so-called marriage. And Carolina looked at me and said, "You remember how he said if he ever hit the lottery the first thing he'd buy would be a Lamborghini where in he would drive one hundred and forty miles an hour?" I said uh-huh and she went ahead and wished it for him, and we buried the note and then she got in the hole and I buried her up to the neck. Carolina and me, we never heard a damn thing about how that turned out. *(Pause.)* Well, maybe we did.

(She EXITS and two actresses ENTER. One playing DARRELL JACKSON moves downstage and kneels facing upstage, holding out roses to the speaker of "True Love.")

TRUE LOVE

ACTRESS. Darrell Jackson, do not start with me again, I mean it. And no more kneeling. Try to remember that I'm an engineer. I am not interested in chocolates, nonsusceptible to roses and I'm immune to valentines. I am post-Byronic. We are at least two generations too late for this. Don't moon at me. Love was perfectly all right before we got cable and E-Bay; it was the claustrophobic response to limited choice and a dearth of useful activities. There was apparently nothing to do but hang around making puppy faces...it's a pre-credit card event. Stop it, Darrell, you stop it...God I hate it when you kiss my feet. Darrell, sit up and listen to me...stop being so insecure, I'm not saying you're not attractive in a sort of Disney style. You have very nice abs, and I admire your pectoralis major but I can pretty much get anything like that I want down at the gym. See me, Darrell, as I really am. I've done polling. I am not a very interesting person: I'm not creative, I'm marginally curious, I don't play a musical instrument, I have no politics, food and wine bore me and I don't understand fashion. What on earth is there to be in love with? I'm interested in architectural stress factors and wiring. Get the lilies away from me! Look at me. Not like that. There is no me for you to dote on. Stop. What do they put on the Valentine cards, Darrell? Poetry is what you find there. There are lies and there are damn lies and anyone who ever bought one of those cards knows it. Do not mistake me, I enjoy our occasional friction between two epidermal layers. Please, Darrell, stop rhyming and swirling your metaphorical cape, and let's behave like the functional inter-gender economic unit the country needs. I know, get your car keys and we'll go buy a home to keep the economic indicators on the up tick. Think of us as predictors in the crucial 28 to 45 technological market range. Come on, big boy, the consumer index gets me hot. Let's roll.

(Four actresses line up equidistant from each other upstage, face the audience and "breathe." The fifth moves downstage to do "Breath.")

BREATH

ACTRESS. Not bad at all. Really good. Keepers, we would call you keepers...the other actresses and myself...concerning you...in your capacity as an audience. We find you...giving, spontaneous... very intelligent, very intelligent, willing to laugh, very important, amazingly important. We...we actresses, together, well we have worked with, what...many, many audiences. I don't know if you know we judge and compare you. We do. The critics analyze us; we analyze you. Afterwards we, you know, have a beer or a, uh...a cranberry juice, and we go over you with a fine tooth comb...no, really, we do, we pick you apart concerning your skills and deportment. Affectionately. I'm not saying it isn't affectionate. And you'll do well. This audience gets good reviews...except...I don't even know if I should bring this up. Should I bring this up? *(The other actresses reply "sure"; "go for it"; "your call"; etc.)* Okay. You're not breathing. You're forgetting to breathe. Breathing is your responsibility as an audience. See, when you're breathing, you're in a receptive state, your senses and intellect take in, but when you don't breathe, you are rejecting... experience... denying it. See, that would be bad for us, bad for the narrative. We would hate that. Right? *(Other actresses say "yes ma'am"; "absolutely"; "you tell 'em, Sister.")* When you breathe, you are aware of the world that is not yourself. It's the reminder that you exist in-relation-to. You recognize yourself, you recognize the other, which closes the circle and creates... well... coherence. It's a big job. If you remembered to breathe, you would do it 14,880 times a day. Not breathing would, practically speaking, mean you were dead, which kind of means doing a play for you would be...well beside the point. *(Sudden awareness.)* Shoot! Can you believe it? I forgot to breathe. I forgot to breathe even though I was talking about breath. Bummer. I was worried that you would think this doesn't belong in a play and, while I did that, you disappeared and I disappeared and all that was present was worry. Terrible. That's terrible of me. I mean to communicate the play I would have to be present. Whoa! Let's go back on track here. Breathe in. Breathe out. Breathe in, breathe out. Breathe in, breathe out. Ah. See, now the play's between us. Breathe again. Oh, that's much better. *(Turns to the next actress.)* Say the next line.

(Actress doing "Spray" immediately says "Harold." All the other actresses EXIT. During the course of "Spray," the speaker mimes

undressing but in fact removes no clothes whatever. At the end she is "naked.")

SPRAY

ACTRESS. Harold? Can you hear me? Do you think it would be possible to have a shower installed, darling? A lovely, roomy shower? My family have never been bath people. Granny Wellfleet said that taking a bath felt like being prepared as the soup course. Harold? You wouldn't call me vain, would you, Harold? Self-involved possibly but not vain. In the tub, I am far, far too conscious of my imperfections. I mean, I'm quite sleek standing up, really, quite aerodynamic, just enough skin so that form follows function.On vacation you always seem to find a reason to seek me out in the shower. Not that I mind, I'm quite flattered really. In the tub, however, unexpected folds are revealed. In a tub I feel more like a hippopotamus or a Shar Pei. And the posture, the posture demanded is unattractive. It's not a lull or a lounge, it's more of a slump really. You do find me beautiful, don't you, Harold? You do fantasize about me, don't you? I so aspire to be a fantasy. It hasn't all been ruined by this hellish tub, has it? Assure me, comfort me, Harold. When painters paint women bathing, they are always standing in pools near waterfalls. Well, Degas contradicts. Ugh. Women by ugly tubs all foldy and blotchy with terrible posture. What could he have been thinking? We could renew our vows in a shower, Harold. Well, I mean, we'd only invite family, of course. Hmmm. If we did that, I suppose the pastor would have to be in the shower with us. It would have to be, I suppose, a rather special pastor. I suppose we could find one on the Internet. You would look perfectly lovely in a shower, Harold. It would emphasize your height and length and curly hair and...elasticity. So it's decided then? All in favor of a shower? Excellent. Please come in, Harold. If you close your eyes you can soap me up.

(One actress ENTERS from each side and hold up beach towels so the "Spray" actress can EXIT modestly. The actress doing "Class War" enters wearing a designer pant suit with "good" jewelry. She fixes her make-up as she speaks.)

CLASS WAR

ACTRESS. Please don't take this personally, but someone in my neighborhood is defacing my SUV. I mean really. This is, is it not, Philadelphia, and not some, well forgive me, hick town where the Herefords and Angus outnumber the lawyers? I exit my home Tuesday the fifteenth at 6:45 AM, as always, and there...there is white paint splattered all over my black SUV. It looked like a Dalmatian only with the negative reversed. First I am shocked and then sad, and then I am outraged, thus I rush in, get an old T-shirt and, as the paint hasn't set yet, I get it off with a little thinner. Fine. College kids or something. Darling teenagers taking out their sexual angst on a powerful object. Next morning, superglue with red paint added. Like measles. Excuse me, I am a well educated single business person, and the world, assuming you are reading the paper, is a very, very dangerous place. I need sanctuary. *(A pause.)* So, I'm out there by dawn's early light taking off the glue with a razor blade and I scratched the car. Scratch the car! Oh, you can imagine I'm happy now. Lyrical. Home is my hideout but the hours I work I'm never home, so the SUV is a moving sanctuary. I decorated it. I have knick knacks in there and a reading light. Some lunch hours I repair there and nap in it. Yes, seen in a certain light you could construe it as symbolic of power and privilege, but that is never said about those ghastly mobile homes. It is a warm, cozy, deeply personal retreat that coincidentally can safely negotiate a freeway. Fine. I stay up all night watching from under a rhododendron. Around 3 AM, a gentleman pulls up in a vehicle so eccentric that it must be an electric car and spray-paints "class war" on my sanctuary. He leaves, I follow him. He stops at a stoplight, I hit the gas and I run over his car. I don't mean to say I hit his car, I roll up and over the top of it like a speed bump. He crawls out and I see he is unfortunately unhurt, so I back up and give him a little "whack," which I feel will be instructive. Attend. An intruder in your home you can shoot. My SUV is a home. Ergo, I give him a little whack. The gentleman was probably an environmentalist, right? I find that quite admirable insofar as they stick to the trees. Now, dear sir, I come out of the store and find you peering in my driver's side window and, intuiting your politics, I say to you one thing and one thing only... "back away from the car!"

(She glares for a moment and then EXITS. Two actresses ENTER. One knocks on an imaginary door. This is Suzi. The one who ENTERS is the speaker for "Twinkies.")

TWINKIES

ACTRESS. Oh, wow. Suzi, hi. Ummm. No, I'm not, well, busy exactly, I'm...oh, you brought me...it's uh...what is that? Oh, it's a casserole. Wow. I thought casseroles were, gosh, extinct. Actually this is incredibly perfect. I love casseroles, they're so comfortingly lumpy. Ummm. Listen Suzi, I'm not really sick...not really...I've been saying I have the flu and, as you see, staying home from work...actually Jack is staying home too, we're...Suzi, can I trust you...my heavens, I've trusted you since elementary school...see, actually we're regressing. We stayed home to regress. Yup. We're playing Twister. Jack's hit green three times in a row, it's hysterical. When we finish Twister, we're going to play with my Strawberry Shortcake dolls

SEZ SHE

and have whole milk and fig newtons. You look confounded or...gosh, actually you look appalled. It's worse than you think, before Twister we were trading Care Bears cards and listening to the Chipmunks. You could come in. Do you have any Barbies or Star Wars action figures? Listen, it's a desperate search for forgotten pleasure. The newspaper is all genocide all the time. T.V. is cop shows, movies are all drug murders, and what can we do? How can we fix it? Everyday I feel guilty about mass starvation, displaced populations and innocent prisoners who have no D.N.A. tests. Dead horses. Dead civilians. Jack and I were depressed all the time. We didn't make love anymore, we just shared guilt. Anytime we took a breath, we just obsessed on the fact that we had personally done nothing to improve air quality or stop global warming...what is global warming anyway? How do I know, we're probably making it worse right now. We'd run through all the mood stabilizers. Twice. Now we play hooky from work. We watch Sesame Street and eat Juju-Bees. We tried to play Battleship but we couldn't remember the number of cruisers. We're just cogs. Very small cogs, but everything conspires to make us feel responsible. We had to stop. We had to give up being crushed by the weight of unassumable responsibility. Trying to be mature and functional was a bad dream, completely unrealistic. The reality is that "Hello Kitty" is our natural level and, within the structure of Twister, we're quite competent. Come on in. Bring your casserole. It's my 35th birthday. Want to have Twinkies with us? Come on in.

(The two actresses EXIT. Two others ENTER carrying a kitchen table. A third actress brings a chair and sits at the table snapping beans, either real or imaginary. This is the speaker for "Beans.")

BEANS

ACTRESS. I like snapping beans with you, Mama. I like being back in the kitchen. I like the top of this old wooden table. You know, Mama, sometimes you suddenly understand. You understand fully and profoundly, bang, just like that. Yesterday, in my kitchen, a short time after breakfast, I understood that I enjoy a more intimate connection with my Labrador retriever than with my husband. My husband, Carl, the Lutheran car mechanic, is entirely opaque. His mind is like a shiny surface where you may find yourself reflected but never invited. You want some more coffee? Carl is an "uh-huh" man. He always answers positively, he always agrees, and meanwhile the dark ship of what he really thinks sails away up heavily forested rivers you will never know. Carl wishes only that I make his life less complex, create a stable environment where, like a Petri dish, he can grow his implacable fantasies like molds in a damp place. Oh, this is good. I love any coffee that isn't mine. See, to live with Carl I must live inside his parameters, and because they are small and tight and unforgiving, they are sort of soul binding in the manner of ancient Chinese foot-wrapping and, like those feet, I am being inexorably deformed, squeezed into shapes and behaviors I could never have imagined. Oh, I dream of escape bur really it is far too late because, you see, now if I removed the bindings I would find my deformity perfectly, exquisitely formed for only one thing. Why, life with Carl, of course. I would be suitably framed for nothing else. All done. How are you doing, Mama. You still got that eye dryness?

(The actress doing "Fly Me to The Moon" speaks immediately. She wears a red or primary colored short cocktail dress. Showy would describe it. As she begins, two actresses ENTER and remove the table, and a third the chair. The actress speaking takes

no notice of them.)

FLY ME TO THE MOON

ACTRESS. Hey, Joey? Come take a look at this. Joey?! I need an opinion here. I'm thinking like this might be, you know, like too revealing. Too much leg maybe, too much...and here I might be flattering myself, too much, you know, cleavage. Joey, come on, I'm kind of out of my depth here because I never visited a prison before. Listen, Joey, it's a delicate balance, right. I want your brother to feel, you know, that as a fiancé you've made, you know, a good choice. Not only have you selected a high school graduate but a tasteful and, let's not leave out, desirable person. You think I'm a desirable person, right Joey? On the other hand, please, I don't want to be an erotic distraction to a buncha wild animals in the big house! So, like Joey, I'm on the horns of a dilemma if you follow me here. To shawl or not to shawl. That is the question. Five-inch heels or three-inch heels. And what am I to think concerning perfume? Joey, you in the bathroom? I'm putting on some kiss-me-lipstick, just a fashion accent. Was it thirteen of fourteen bank robberies your brother pulled off? I'm going to characterize that as illegal though the guy was just trying to feed his family, right? Okey-dokey, so I think this is the ensemble. Very, very definitely. You listening, Joey? What I respect in your brother, and I'm serious here...maybe no eye shadow...is that he never ratted on his watchamacallit, co-conspirator, who drove the getaway car. Right, Joey? Hey, it's all about loyalty, I'm not kidding. You respect that, right, Joey? The guy they said was 5'10", one hundred sixty, slight limp...the guy who always whistled Sinatra records. *(A pause.)* Hey, Joey, could you come in here for a minute?

(She EXITS. The actress doing "Sex" ENTERS. She is wearing

pajamas.)

SEX

ACTRESS. Sex. Hmmm. Men think about it every 17 seconds, women every 41 seconds. *(Looks at watch.)* I think I'm exceeding my average. I don't know why it's so important to us, do you? It must be a genetic need for abandon. It causes so much trouble. Of course, if it wasn't a possibility it would be the end of high school reunions. If you do sex well, it results in the "wheeeee" effect, and, of course, it's the "wheeeee" effect that makes us think about sex every 41 seconds. Men apparently need more "wheeeee!" *(Looks at watch.)* Oh dear, I apologize for taking you past the 41-second limit. I know, let's close our eyes and think about it together. All closed? Good. The woman in pink in the second row, you're not concentrating. Isn't this fun? Group sex. After 41 seconds of complete silence, there will be the two-bell signal you hear on airplanes when you get to the gate. The docking signal. Everyone, one, two, three, think about it. *(About twenty seconds of silence.)* Whoever gets there first, say "wheeeeeee." *(Twenty more seconds — there is the two-bell signal.)* Boy, we better see a therapist.

SEZ SHE

Act II

(As the lights come up, we see all five actresses on stage wearing a similar color. It would be nice if it were red, but it could be anything. There is no attempt for these quintuplets to all wear the same thing, however. They could be a mix of sitting and standing, as the director requires. At least one actress should wear a red dress she can dance in. While the other actresses change into their other clothes during the course of Act II, this actress remains in the red dress for "Dance," which closes the play.)

QUINTUPLETS. The Morningside quintuplets
SUE. People were
JOAN. Pretty darn
ELLEN. Excited
QUINTUPLETS. When we were born
DORA. Probably because
KIKI. Of a deeply personal
SUE. But nationwide sense
JOAN. Of profound
ELLEN. Belief
QUINTUPLETS. That they weren't our parents
DORA. So we grew up in
KIKI. The brutal glare of

SUE. Intense
JOAN. Media scrutiny
ELLEN. With front page coverage when we
DORA. For instance
QUINTUPLETS. Got our periods
KIKI. And
SUE. This resulted
JOAN. In a fanatical
ELLEN. Ferocious
DORA. Unparalleled
QUINTUPLETS. Desire for privacy
KIKI. Which led us to
SUE. Practice holding our breath
JOAN. For
ELLEN. Long periods of time
DORA. So that we
KIKI. Could stay at the bottom
SUE. Of the family swimming pool
JOAN. When reporters
ELLEN. Showed up.
DORA. We got up to
QUINTUPLETS. Nine minutes
KIKI. Actually
QUINTUPLETS. Which we didn't realize was unusual
SUE. Until
JOAN. One day
ELLEN. When we were checking our lipstick
QUINTUPLETS. We noticed
DORA. That we were
QUINTUPLETS. Growing gills
KIKI. Which was not
SUE. Considered cool

JOAN. In middle school
ELLEN. So we spent a lot of time
DORA. In detention
KIKI. Which was followed by
SUE. Scales
JOAN. And
ELLEN. Tails
DORA. So that in high school
KIKI. It was pretty clear
SUE. That we were becoming
JOAN. In point of fact
QUINTUPLETS. Mermaids
ELLEN. Which by our senior year
DORA. Made it absolutely impossible
KIKI. To continue as
QUINTUPLETS. Cheerleaders
SUE. So that as a lifestyle choice
JOAN. We pretty much abandoned land and
ELLEN. Became resident in
DORA. The Pacific Ocean
KIKI. Where we hung out with
SUE. And became romantically involved with
QUINTUPLETS. Dolphins
JOAN. With whom we subsequently
ELLEN. Made our fortune
DORA. By contriving
KIKI. Five simultaneous marriages
SUE. In a specially built tank
QUINTUPLETS. In a Las Vegas chapel
JOAN. Thus pioneering
ELLEN. Interspecies parenting and sexuality
QUINTUPLETS. Which as others have taken it up

SEZ SHE

DORA. Has led to
KIKI. Incredibly increased
SUE. Environmental awareness
JOAN. And peace on earth
ELLEN. Where so few humans
QUINTUPLETS. Continue to reside
DORA. So to those of you who are
KIKI. *(Gesturing toward the audience.)* Still holding out
QUINTUPLETS. The Morningside Quintuplets would like to say

SUE. You just have no idea of
JOAN. The life-changing quality
ELLEN. And ineffable pleasure
DORA. Of multiple orgasms
QUINTUPLETS. With a shark.

(At the end of the piece, four actresses leave the stage; two of them for a change out of red. The remaining actress should not be the one who closes the play with "Dance.")

REDSHIFT

ACTRESS. Do you know what redshift is? In the 1920's, a redshift was observed in the light coming from the Andromeda Nebula... meaning that the light's frequency is shifted toward the red in the spectrum, which indicates that its source is moving away from us, and that's what I'm experiencing in things and people and events. A redshift even in myself, a sense that I'm moving away from me, a feeling I'm leaving myself behind, a sense of growing smaller and less important in my own perception, as in a diminishment. A diminished Sarah. All the people I love have this red aureole. My parents moving away from me into extreme old age, my husband moving away from intimacy, my son moving away into his own life, my profession, real estate, moving away as it loses meaning and necessity for me, until I fear I shall shortly disappear and that on cloudy, wet days like today I should even instigate it. Do the simple magic trick that would let me disappear. If you think of a balloon with dots drawn on its surface, well, as it was inflated, a person, me, sitting on only one of the dots would see every other dot moving away and, though I would think I was the stable center of the universe, that would not be true because, in reality, I would be moving away from other dots at the same speed and in the same scale. So the redshift I suffer is yours as well. I think of redshift as the light we give off burning away until we all become dead reflective moons. I'm sorry, I should be more cheerful. I see that, even while I've been talking, you moved away. I can feel it. I'm smaller. Redshift.

(At the end of "Redshift", all the actors return. Perhaps someone with chalk draws a square the size of an elevator and then all five actresses scrunch into it. Once all are inside the square, "Between Floors" begins.)

BETWEEN FLOORS

ACTRESS. Really, I'm not very fond of being stuck in this elevator. I mean you're all very nice people and, if I had to choose five people I'd like to fall 47 floors to my death with, well, you'd be in the finals. I mean I might choose people with better snacks, but, putting that aside, you're a nice range of body types. How long have we been in here now? Five hours? We've been in here five hours? And how many breakdowns have I had so far? Really? Well, that's not so bad. Feel one coming on though. Feel that little jingle jangle that means panic's on the way. Actually it's kind of interesting to have all my phobias interact and coalesce in one very small space so that

SEZ SHE

I'm not just experiencing fear, it's fear squared. I'm afraid of heights, I'm claustrophobic, I'm afraid of death and I'm petrified of the dark, so this is really perfect for me. What I think I'm going to do is release some tension by screaming. Everybody cool with that? Yup, I can feel it coming. Yup, it's almost here! They once had a bloodcurdling scream contest in my sorority and you guess who won? All right, I'm losing control now, my gorge is rising, I'm losing any rational sense of my surroundings, my head is swimming, please don't any of you take this seriously...oh my God... *(She emits a piercingly loud, endless scream.)* Okay, I'm going to do one more. *(She does.)* Hope I haven't raised the stress level. *(She screams again.)* There, now I'm ready to assist others with their problems and feelings. I'm completely calm and ready to deal with our crisis. The most important thing, as we all know, is to remain calm and keep a positive attitude. *(She screams even louder than before.)* Sorry, that one caught me by surprise.

(A moment, then four of the actresses scatter offstage. There should, by the way, be a change out of red for another actress, leaving only two in the red tones the act began in. Someone hands the actress speaking "Date" several books. This actor pursues an unseen professor across the stage.)

DATE

ACTRESS. Professor Drysdale? Professor Drysdale? I'm terribly sorry to come puffing up to you all out of breath like this, but I had a question about Rome, really. I'm not keeping you from class, am I? Oh good. I would hate to be a nuisance. I'm not imposing, am I? Oh, double good. You see I seem to have lost or incorrectly discarded or mistakenly eaten my January 17th notes, and I'm completely flummoxed as to whether it was Scipio or Cato who died in exile? Oh good, Scipio, right, well that clears that right up, I was so flummoxed. Wait, Professor Drysdale, one more question, just one, I promise. I wondered if we'd be taking off our clothes again anytime soon? I'm not speaking too loudly, am I? Because if we were, if that was on the schedule, I think I'd like to be conscious this time. Just for the experience. Because that drink you gave me, well, I just wasn't really aware of all the fun we must have had after that, and now that I've been *(How did Curio the Younger put it?)* deflowered, I was hoping to be present the next time, and get the full effect. Hi, Sally, hi, Alexander! Oh really? No, I don't think I can make it to the study group because as far as I know, Professor Drysdale here will be sexually harassing me this evening. I know, he looks kind of old and wizened, but that doesn't matter because, luckily he has knockout drops which skims us right past the age difference. Bye. So I could probably meet you around six because I have a meeting with Dean Montgomery at four, nothing academic, just a little personal problem, but it won't take too long. So, anyway, we could discuss the aqueducts and Hadrian, and then you could take advantage of me, which might get a little kinky because I'll be wired this time. Bye, Professor Drysdale. Can't wait. See you. Bye. Quo Vadis.

(She EXITS with the books. Three actresses wearing Pinocchio noses ENTER. Two stand in the back facing the audience, the third sits in a simple wooden chair painted with sunflowers.)

TRUTH OR CONSEQUENCES

ACTRESS. *(A woman whose nose is growing a la Pinocchio.)* So I took my five-year-old to see Pinocchio and now this. I have no idea why; maybe there was a virus in the theatre. Disney has a lot of money, maybe they're experimenting on us. It turns out there were 37 adults at the showing, and every one of us has the condition. At least the children and the troop of cub scouts were spared. Hell yes, we're suing everybody. *(Touches her nose.)* It expands and contracts. It's this way because I told my mother Dennis and I couldn't wait to come to dinner. Today wasn't good: a grocery check-out girl asked me if I died my hair, my boss asked my age and my husband asked if I loved him...I had to spend the rest of the day with my nose propped up on the kitchen island. God forbid I commit adultery or my children ask if I've smoked marijuana. I suppose you're so honest you don't have to worry? Frankly, this makes social interaction impossible. I never realized how dependent we all are on tact. What if this is the forerunner of the Government letting this stuff loose in the water system like fluoride? They certainly wouldn't need the F.B.I. or the C.I.A. It's not funny. My husband laughed for about a week, but now he's living at his sister's. Everybody wonders, is it communicable? I can clear an entire P.T.A. meeting when I sneeze. I knew the world was coming to an end but I never guessed it was because of Gepetto. I have advice for you — flee the theatre.

(She sneezes. The speaker EXITS as does one of the two background Pinocchios. The other hands off her nose and takes off her coat, revealing a really "cute" outfit, perhaps anchored by an angora sweater. There should be "cute" music behind this next piece. Perhaps she could start "Workshop" carrying a darling puppy and then hand it off.)

WORKSHOP

ACTRESS. Hi there! How are you doing? Looking good! Everybody's on a happiness jag, right? I know I am. Welcome to our three-day personal workshop in post-feminist cute. More importantly, can you and should you be it? Should you choose to sparkle? Cuddly, bouncy, silly and adorable. Can you get into it?

SEZ SHE

Let's get down. Sparkle is awareness, what I call the "acute sense of being," and as Martin Heidigger believed, awareness leads to anxiety, a dread of nothingness in a groundless world, and, Honey, you don't want to be there, don't want to do that! See, we can only stave that off by absorbing ourselves in shallow and mundane concerns, and that, let me tell you, is where cute comes in. Do not, I say do not give in to the malicious categorization of the unknowing. "Cute" is not a degradation, not a lack of moral seriousness, but is, more specifically, an act of aesthetic optimism in the midst of existential distress. "Sparkle," you sweet things, is not subjective, it must be apprehended to exist, which, need I say, is the opposite of solipsism, which makes subjective experience the basis of knowledge. "Cute" is a philosophic choice which validates the other and thus builds community, which is our greatest need, so Honey, you don't have to take any more shit about this. Get loose, Honey! For three dynamic days you are gonna bounce, squeal, giggle and charm your way out of the existential dilemma and, thus, as Sartre said, "Find your essence and become complete." Are you excited? Boy, I am! Do you dare to be fluffy? Can you wrinkle up your nose when you smile? You bet your patooty you can! We are gonna start by the whole room thinking of itself as a dimple. And-a-one, and-a-two, and-a-three, sparkle!

(She taps or soft-shoes her way off as a lectern is pushed on. The actress performing "Valedictorian" moves behind the lectern in the traditional cap and gown.)

VALEDICTORIAN

ACTRESS. Ummm...ummm...do I have my...good, okay, yeah...got that...ummm...honored...sorry, sorry...Governor, ummm Clark...honored...shoot, I dropped...there...guests, honored guests...ummm, you know, parents, students...well, actually, faculty, parents and uh...and uh...did I say parents? I said parents...so anyway...oh, students, the other one was students...faculty, parents, students...so that's uh, that's everybody right? Pretty much everybody and...notes, I have notes here, index cards...well, I was pretty sure I...okay, I don't...my notes aren't...where could I...gee, without notes I...kitchen table, kitchen table...no notes. No notes. Valedictorian. Complete surprise to me and uh...and uh...doubtless to you. To you. Kinda lost my train of...oh, surprised to be...can you hear me? Is this on? Whoa, feedback. Whoa, okay it's, it's on, right? So that's good, that's a good thing. Honored guests. I did that, right? Itchy. Sorry. Ummm. As we set forth, ummm, proceed outward... begin... *(Stops and looks at the audience.)* Everybody all right out there? Looking a little blank, a little frozen. Whoa. Where was I? Did I do the venturing out part? No? Okay. Nothing ventured, nothing gotten. *(Knows "gotten" isn't the word.)* Had. Received. No, obtained. Gained! Nothing gained. Nothing ventured, nothing gained. *(Pause.)* You know I really have no advice for you. Go out there, do whatever, mess around...whatever's coming down the pike...get lucky, that's my advice. How the hell did I ever get into this? Okay, okay, ummm, anyway you know...listen, to hell with it. You know what I mean? *(Pause.)* Right?

(She stands for a few seconds in silence and then abruptly walks off. As she goes, a woman enters in a long-sleeved blouse. Her face and hands are green.)

COLOR

ACTRESS. I did this for an environmental protest, and it didn't come off. There are eleven hundred of us actually. We're called the Huntsville, Alabama Thousand. My suspicion is that the person who pro-

vided the makeup to the rally was a government agent. Or maybe
not. Obviously it could be the pharmaceutical companies. Or my
half-sister Gala who dislikes me intensely. The point is we are now
people of color. Eleven hundred of us. We are America's newest
minority group. Some people just call us greens, but we prefer the
term Forest- Americans. It's been three years now. Seventy-six percent of us have lost our jobs since then. We seem particularly unwelcome in banking. Well, corporate law and catering, those haven't
been working out. My father, who is African-American, took me
aside and asked if I wouldn't be happier with my own kind. My
boyfriend finally said he was leaving. He said it wasn't because I
was green, it was just my particular shade. I mean, I'm a pretty dark
green. Then some people started using the P word. It's the one thing
Forest-Americans can't stand. The right-wing groups started it, they
called us Pukie. I'm green and I'm proud. It's easier if we stick
together. The biggest issue is whether or not to dye our children.
Personally I want green children. Go outside and look around, it's
natural. I want my children to be part of the predominant color in
nature. Most of us are vegetarians as a political choice. Naturally,
there's a lot of masked racism too. For instance, people say, oh yes,
they're brilliant gardeners and incredibly wonderful duck hunters.
We get offered a lot of lawn work. Am I angry? Yes, I'm angry. It's
not easy to change your race at my age. Sure, I wish I was part of
the dominant culture, but there are nights when I'm down at the
Chlorophyll Gospel Church in the midst of those powerful voices
rockin' out "Mother Nature, Bring Me Home" that I wouldn't want
to be any other color. White, black, Hispanic, Asian, you guys will
never know what it means to be deciduous. Call me a Pukie if you
will, spring will never mean to you what it means to me.

*(She EXITS. A desk is rolled on and a chair. A woman ENTERS
talking on a mobile phone. She sits. Another woman ENTERS.*

SEZ SHE

The woman at the desk notices her and "Medoff" begins.)

MEDOFF

ACTRESS. Ah, Jackson, delighted you could stop by my office. You needed a decision on Medoff, yes? Hmmm. Well, let's frame the question, shall we? Can a centrally significant executive allow a family problem priority over his corporate responsibilities and retain a highly remunerated position? You see, I fear not. Let's frame an answer. Such remuneration implies unlimited availability whether that be dawn, evening, weekends, holidays, whenever necessary. The primacy of business obligations, a given in corporate culture, eh, Jackson? As Team Leader you were cognizant of Medoff's dilemma, a desperately ill wife...dying actually, and naturally we share his profound concern, his grief. Let's frame the evidence, Jackson. He missed meetings to bathe her, appointments to read to her, he has cancelled client dinners or sent subordinates in his stead. Hmmm. Good for a day Jackson, a week, but a month? Dear me I fear not. He was seen to weep in a merger meeting. A chief financial officer weeping in the boardroom? Hmmm. He then took 21 days of personal time during the press of year-end business. We then conveyed a generous offer of reassignment, albeit for less money, which he rather brusquely refused to discuss. Bad form. Let's frame a decision, shall we, Jackson? I have taken the responsibility of preparing and in fact mailing a letter of termination in which I regretfully itemized his unacceptable priorities, and informed him that he owed us fiduciary duties which he had clearly breached. I understand that tragically his wife passed away on the day he received our letter, which is, as I'm sure you agree, Jackson, damned bad luck. Your need for a decision is thus, I fear, after the fact. I think we may safely call the principle invoked here as inviolable, and the matter closed. Now, Jackson, you had something to discuss concerning your daughter. Please sit down.

(A moment. The actress and the furniture clear. On the bare stage a woman in 18th Century court dress ENTERS.)

THE BEDCHAMBER

ACTRESS. Ah, your majesty... *(A deep curtsy.)* Pray forgive an interruption so late, but Lord Montgomery had intimated you might not find my presence entirely unwelcome, that I might be considered an adornment or, shall I say, a cherishment on such a cold night in Your Highness's bedchamber, and so I have risked chastisement for my appearance here so long after vespers, acting as one might say on whim or impulse in the hope that that which your glorious ascendancy would, in fact, most dear Monarch, not prove to be my undoing but rather a peccadillo of some charm that you might find infinitesimally amusing and not beneath such a great one's inclined consideration, which I entreat not be seen or thought to contain dark seeds of personal advancement, an indelicate ruse to rise but more simply a courteous attraction and understanding that, as the Queen is currently arrayed in Canterbury in close, might one say, intimate association with his magnificence, the Archbishop, that you might in your momentary solitude desire a sympathetic ear, let us say an inclinement from one considered not entirely loathsome to the eye, rough to the touch or incapable of a pretty abandon when found in dishabille, as I now, beribboned and blushing, appear before you, and I might hope you would but deign to disengage this single ivory button, revealing to your most august eye a pretty confusion caused by my unpracticed surprise at the royal engagement which one should not but notice Your Majesty display upon my arrival. *(A curtsy to the floor.)* Your servant, Sir.

SEZ SHE

*(The Lady EXITS. It would be perfect if the next piece were filmed
and shown in simple close-up. If not, someone holds a T.V. frame
in front of the actress doing "Don't Look." A special lights her
face.)*

DON'T LOOK

ACTRESS. Can I tell you something embarrassing? No, don't look
at me. No, don't. This thing that is embarrassing is that you make
me happy. It's embarrassing because it's too old fashioned. I should
be wearing gingham or riding in a carriage or something. I should
be talking about self-actualization or professional advancement or
finding thousands of dollars of drug money in an old paper bag, but
it's just you, just your presence, just your slow smile. I couldn't
place the feeling at first, I thought maybe I was sleepy or had a low
grade fever, and I asked my sister if I looked pale, and she said "No,
actually, you look happy," and I laughed and said "Oh, right," because it felt comfortable being cynical, but then I sat out on the old
rocker on the porch and kind of checked myself out internally, and I
had to get over myself and admit I was recognizably happy, and it
was your fault. So, thank you, because it hasn't happened to me
very often and, of course, I can't be sure of the duration but I'm sure
of where it comes from...you. So, I guess you could look at me
now...if you wanted to...if you wanted to see what happy looked
like. Stop smiling.

*(She EXITS. A woman in strip mall chic ENTERS with a beer in
hand. She is used to being considered both sexy and tough. If
she sits on anything, it would be a bar stool.)*

STUCK

ACTRESS. Ummm, me an' Mookie, he's my, whatchacallit, boy-friend, well, sort of, anyway we went out...we was goin' to pair up with Sheanna, my friend Sheanna, but her fiancé — which is a laugh, them both bein' like high school freshmen — hadda work doin' ice repair an' stuff like that down at the rink where he has a weekend gig..so Mookie says like "whatever," an' we say later to Sheanna, who is completely bummed but she doesn't want to go drivin' which is Mookie's idea, so me an' Mookie just split an' we hit the six-plex, but the movies are like monster flicks an' martial junk, which is just not anything I'm into, so what's the deal? You know what I mean. So Mookie takes the Willhasset Parkway east to Seaconga exit an' tries puffin' over by this, I don't know, dump place. Starts stickin' his hands into where I'm not interested, 'cause it's like 8:30 or even less an' it's not, you know, cool to be doin' any sex before, I don't know, at least eleven, for hell's sake. Well, maybe ten on a week-night. So I say, Mookie, looky here, you got dirty fingernails an' you ain't touchin' me here, there or anywhere till you go over them things with a brush an' some sani-scrub, so you better lay us some rubber or you ain't getting' any from me all night. Well, he's stuck in the mud. I ain't kiddin'. See, he pulled off in the soft by this dump thing an' he don't have no four-wheel drive an' no matter how he rocks it, we just sinking' in an' I say, oh, fine. Oh, this is just real good. Like I'm gonna call my dad say come get us out to the dump thing, which he don't like Mookie anyway, an' what the hell are we parkin' seein' as how it's still half daylight and "you're grounded all week," which is what he'd probably say. So, I'm givin' Mookie some real pissy responses up one side an' down the other, an' there comes this rappin' on the window. Well, it's this bum...no, really...all half dirty with teeth some yellow color you never saw, says looks like we're stuck, an' Mookie says hell, yeah, we're stuck, an' he says looks like we were cuttin' off a piece an' Mookie says we weren't cuttin' off no piece, an' he says, oh, yeah, well he'd like to get in on that, so Mookie kills him. Well, Mookie, he has a temper, you know what I mean. Mookie shoots him through the window with his daddy's gun he don't even know Mookie has. An' I say, "Well, hell Mookie," an' we get out an' drag this guy up the dump, weighin' about 200 pounds, an' put him in the trunk this '84 Impala barely stickin' out the dump place, an' we stick boards under Mookie's tires an' get on out. Wash up at the Sonoco and, hell, there's Sheanna, says Bobby done at the ice rink so we go get us a turkey pepperoni pizza, which is a special, which we don't hardly like, so we go off somewhere let 'em put their hands on us a little an' they split for midnight football, so me an' Sheanna go back to her mom's, who is passed out, so we get the Colt 40s in the fridge, which is about the best thing all night by a mile. So, that's all. That's the murder we done two years back, but it was only this bum out to rape an' whatever, an' there ain't too many people go to the dump place an' Mookie, well, he joined up the Marines an' I never did tell Sheanna 'cause she got a big mouth so that was jus' a chapter of my growin' up, though I have learned to shoot since then lest I should ever get molested, so it all turned out all right. I don't think about it. I don't know why I thought about it now. Jus' a high school thing. You got those memories yourself, don'tcha? Sure you do. Some people say that's the best time of your life.

(She kills the beer, tosses it offstage and EXITS the other direction. A woman who knows she is beautiful ENTERS. She reclines on something or other.)

MANNEQUIN

ACTRESS. Mirror, mirror, on the wall, who's the fairest one of all?

SEZ SHE

Yes, I know I am. It is said that I exemplify, well, actually, embody the Grecian ideal of the feminine. They measured seven statues of Venus emerging from the sea, and those are my measurements. Believe me, I'm not bragging. I used to weigh two hundred and ten pounds. I had a beaked nose, a wandering eye and a foreshortened right leg, but I had extreme plastic surgery on a reality show and now I'm a goddess. You know the phrase "stops traffic?" Well, I have literally stopped traffic, I'm told there were multiple injuries. Oh yes, there are problems...teeny tiny ones. No one recognizes me, I frighten my husband, my dog barks at me and I have absolutely no idea who I am. Men consider me unobtainable and women loathe me. I have no privacy. I used to work as a dental assistant but I was fired for being distracting. Reconstituted as I am, it would be fun to wear a bikini but not when you live in Fairbanks, Alaska. I realize now that there are talents necessary to inhabiting beauty, and I don't have them. I don't like being watched for one thing. I'm phobic about people I can't stand being attracted to me. It's my personal opinion that beauty is a one-trick pony. I spend all my time now doing bake sales and car washes to raise the money for the surgeries to put me back the way I was. I know how to be that person. I had a lot of practice, and I didn't have to think about it. I don't even know which side of the bed this person likes to sleep on. My only dream now is to stand in front of the mirror, say the poem and have the mirror laugh.

(She EXITS. Two people ENTER with a five-foot long cartoon version of a classroom blackboard. On it in mockchalk is written "Mrs. Ellington's Fabulous 3rd Grade." Mrs. Ellington ENTERS energetically.)

SCHOOLDAYS

ACTRESS. Good morning, children. Oh, I like that so much when you say my name in unison. It makes Mrs. Ellington feel humble and tingly and ready to make educational magic. Now I know you're just as happy and excited as your Mommy and Daddy that at the very last moment America' s public schools have been saved. Let's cheer. Hip, hip, hooray. Very nicely done, and the clapping at the end was a lovely touch. Yes, Abraham Lincoln Elementary has been saved by our country's nicest and friendliest and largest corporations who have bought us. Yes, you and I and our classroom and even our pencils. Isn't that grand? Now, whenever there is a change in our lives, we wake up the next morning and have the fun of things being a little different. Right? So here's what's different today. You see there's a little straw sticking up from your desk. See it? Now if you sip on that straw, you'll find a very famous cola is fizzing around in your mouth. Isn't that fun? You can do it anytime, even when Mrs. Ellington is teaching, and those little numbers you see moving tell us just how much to bill your parents at the end of the month. Try sipping and see those numbers get bigger. Wow. But there's more. Isn't that lucky? If you get up for a teeny minute, you'll see there is a little rough spot on your chair seat which, without your even knowing, samples fibers in your clothing and, if you're wearing clothes from a very famous clothing chain, all your grades for the day go up five points to help you get an A. Let's applaud that very famous clothing chain. Now when you do get an A, and Mrs. Ellington hopes you always will, the little tiny screen in your desk lights up and you get to see 60 seconds of a new movie that hasn't come out yet that is suitable to your age and experience and, if you bring back the parent's release form, it can even be PG13. For that we're all going to draw a thank-you picture for a very famous media company. Finally, when we're doing our Pledge of Allegiance wearing our new headsets, it's recorded by our very own government, so anybody who doesn't know it perfectly yet can get some extra help and a delicious candy treat at our new C.I.A. center, where the auditorium used to be. Now the fun part is, every teacher you have has other, different fun changes paid for by different famous companies, so if you ask me, the fun never stops. Now, open your books, it's time to study our corporate history.

(She claps twice, smiles at the children and then EXITS. An old woman is pushed on in a wheelchair.)

HOLIDAY

ACTRESS. Hey, Benny, it's time for the celebration! *(To the audience.)* Benny and me, we always celebrate the hour. My point being there's never enough celebration. Birthdays, Christmas, weddings, anniversarys, maybe Thanksgiving. That comes down to about one celebration every two months. Now that's just plain old not enough celebration, life being as short as it is. See what it says on this cake I'm decorating? Happy nine PM. What with three kids, my skin condition, Benny out of work and the alternator shot, when we make it to nine o'clock that's a celebration. We go to bed at ten and we have sparklers after we turn out the light. We get up at five-thirty so we can have presents before we go to work, then we call each other on our lunch breaks just to hoot and holler. It works out pretty well. When I look around, I feel like Benny and me have a better time than most people. We always have a nice big turkey on the microwave's birthday. We celebrate colds, we celebrate income tax, we celebrate garbage day. Make it a little different for each one, you know. Then we have a big celebration on August 15 for Damn Fool's Day which celebrates all these damn fool celebrations. My advice to you is don't just sit around waiting for other people to tell you it's all right to have fun. *(Calls.)* Come on, Benny, you got to cut the nine o'clock cake!

(She gets out of the wheelchair and EXITS. Someone else pushes off the chair. The stage is bare for a moment. A woman in simple mourning ENTERS.)

TARMAC

ACTRESS. They let us out on the runway...out on the tarmac. There were padded folding chairs, maybe fifty or sixty behind stanchions, and velvet ropes, and we sat there, all these people who didn't know each other lost in our own thoughts while we waited for our sons. And what I noticed was that we all had such good posture and that we were so still, so very still. Nine families waiting for nine flag-draped coffins, and all of us sitting up straight as if death had finally gotten our attention. The plane was huge, huge, someone said later they could transport tanks in it, and the back opened and they rolled them out, each coffin on its own pushcart with two attendants, soldiers, and the wheels didn't squeak, they had really good casters, and they rolled, in formation, up to the velvet ropes and all stopped at once in a perfect line, and I wondered who had choreographed this and how it had been described when he was offered the job. Then they removed one of the velvet ropes, and all the silent people with good posture filed past slowly trying not to act surprised that there were no names, that the coffins were all unmarked. And I had bought a little drug store camera on the ride down, and I took it out and snapped a picture because I wanted some final memory of my brother, and a nice looking soldier walked over and smiled and said, "I'm sorry, ma'am, no photographs," and I said it's a personal memory and he nodded and said "I'll have to have your camera, ma'am," and I understood that they were afraid. They were afraid war would get a bad reputation and I couldn't help it, I laughed. And no one turned. No one looked. No one wanted to have that information. So I gave the soldier the camera and I walked on.

(The "Tarmac" speaker EXITS. A woman in a tux or formal dress ENTERS. She comes all the way downstage and surveys the audience. She should light a cigarette with a five dollar bill.)

ME

ACTRESS. My name is Jackie Carmody Wilcox. My social security number is 532-34-1435, my driver's license 072307 and I'm a highly satisfied victim of identity theft. If you get right down to it, from almost any perspective, my identity sucked. Really, you could barely call it an identity. I worked in an office with six people and, when I left after eleven years, one of them had to ask me my last name to put on the gift certificate. A year later my credit card company became alarmed at the sudden increase in my purchases, my bank account was drained and somebody took out a second mortgage on my house. Well, it was clear what had happened. I'm thinking it was the old tax returns that went into my recyclables. I'd kept meaning to get a shredder but it seemed so pretentious. When I looked at that credit card bill, I experienced an indescribable sensation which I will describe to you. The person defined by that bill was...flamboyant. Look at me, I thought, I gambled in Monaco, I lived in five-star hotels in Cairo and Paris. Not only was I an arms dealer and an art collector, I was a passenger on the last flight of the Concorde. I was fascinating, I was dangerous, I wore Versachi. It was the first time in my life I wanted to be me. But the only way to be that me was to track down who was being me, and that was going to take a lot of money. I went to the library and for a month I read everything there was about identity theft. It's not very hard to do.

Amazingly there are magazine articles that lay it out very, very clearly, step by step, in layman's terms. All my life I've been a successful student. In my first week I cleared $7,000 — I won't even tell you what I make now — I stay in luxury hotels in Cairo and Paris, I wear designer dresses, I'm dating an arms dealer, I collect lithographs. No, really I do. Oddly I never found the person who gave me this new identity. The me who got away. But you see it matters not at all because I am that me. I live it. I revel in it. Have fantasies. Be them.

(The "Me" speaker EXITS. A woman in a coach's garb ENTERS. She speaks for a line or two through a bullhorn.)

SYNCHRONIZED EATING

ACTRESS. Awright, awright, listen up! Fork down, spoon down, gimme your full attention! You, sharrup! That's better, awright, I'm writing this on the blackboard. I am Coach Marilyn Gatullo, newly appointed here at the University of Michigan as head of the women's freshman synchronized eating team. Gatullo, double "L." It is I who led the unheralded, unranked, and unknown New Orleans College eaters to the Final Four held annually at Mall of America. Ladies, obesity may be seen as a national problem, and the easiest way to change that image was to turn it, under Title Nine, into a University-sanctioned sport. As freshmen, and I'm referring to the recent national study published in The New York Times, you are likely as a dorm resident to gain an average of fifteen pounds in your first year. I say let's do that in pursuit of a national championship. Stop listening to the endless browbeating you get from your mother, your father, your sister and your neighbor here in what I call Diet America. Eighty-two percent...let me repeat that...eighty-two percent of American women have dieted in some form in the last year. You lose ten,

you gain ten, you lose twelve, you gain fourteen, it's the oldest story
ever told: I say lets gain forty and go home next summer with the
nine diamonds set in 18 karat gold on your pinky that says you are
the best synchronized eaters in he world. Your mother will no longer
carp and criticize, your mother will be awestruck. Have you ever
seen eleven women eating eleven deep-fried turkeys in unison? How
about rhythmically peeling a dozen avocadoes and eating them so
that the team throws the seeds over their shoulders in one gesture
and they hit the floor in single click? Now that is major league
synchronized eating! Now, training table six AM sharp for a three-
hour full squad practice. Four PM on the dining field until such time
that I, Coach Marilyn Gatullo, am satisfied that we can eat a wide
range of National dishes as if we were one mouth. We are
handmaidens of rhythmic ingestion, devotees of cooperative culi-
nary communality and we cannot and will not be categorized. Nobody finds a 370 pound N.F.L. lineman anything but an athlete.
(Blows whistle.) Forks! Knives! Center the lobster! Wait for it. Wait
for it. *(Fires a starting pistol.)* Lets get cracking!

*(She EXITS. The woman who has remained in red ENTERS,
dancing to salsa music. It ends. An imaginary man ENTERS.
She listens to him for a moment. It should be noted that each
dance has the appropriate music and the nature of each dance
is up to the director as long as they differ greatly the one from
the other.)*

DANCE

ACTRESS. You would? Delightful. My name is Tina Rowan
Blanchard? And yours? With or without an "H?" Ah. Well, it's ex-
tremely nice of you to ask. *(She and her imaginary partner dance
the tango.)* No, it's my first time in Spain. I find the weather delight-

ful, the architecture intriguing and the men...satisfying. *(She dances the polka.)* No, it's my first time in Germany. I find the train system extraordinary, the food fortifying and the men masterful. *(She dances the "frog" or the "pony.")* No, it's my first time in London. I find the fog cosmetic, the history pervasive and the men...nostalgic. *(She waltz's grandly.)* No, it's my first time in Vienna. I find the chocolate devastating, the politics baroque and the men insinuating. *(She fox-trots awkwardly.)* No, it's my first time in Kansas City. I find the...slaughterhouses efficient, the food...inedible and the men...honey, I don't even want to get into it.

(She EXITS. The light fades out.)

End of Play

APPENDIX

(A homeless woman sits on a blanket on a downtown street, her shopping cart with her belongings close beside her, soliciting people as they pass.)

AMELIE

ACTRESS. Anything will help, sir. Anything will help, ma'am. Trying to get my little daughter back from the state, Mister. I need medical attention for esophageal cancer, sir. I hope to be the first homeless woman to be sent into space, ma'am. Buddy, you broke me, you bought me. Hell. People don't give a shit if the weather's too good. Guess they figure I can live on sunshine. *(Pulls out a battered almanac.)* Sun will set tonight at 9:14. I like to know the planetary alignments. Could you tell me the time, sir? Could you tell me the time, ma'am. Won't give me the time of day. *(She laughs.)* Some people they wouldn't give you the droplets from a sneeze. I said that. *(Refers to a small notebook.)* I been on the streets, what, three years, three months, three days. *(A passerby.)* Just a little money for a dress for a job interview, sir. *(Looks in her hand.)* Canadian dime. I'm Amelie Sunderson Canaday in case you were interested. I call myself a victim of the "too much." I believe myself to be a professor of economics. Goes this way. *(She takes out a small coin purse and dumps it into her hand.)* Dollar's worth of change. Jimmy takes a quarter, Billy takes fifty cents, Audrey takes twenty cents, how much does that leave for Donna, Posy and Amelie? The three of us split the nickel. See what happened here is that Jimmy, Billy and Audrey took too much. Pretty easy to understand, huh? *(Rises.)* I got to get ready for bed. See that stray dog over there? Shepherd mix by the garbage can? I kill dogs like that an eat 'em. I got a machete for that. Not tonight though, I splurged on cat food. *(She takes out a pack of*

SEZ SHE

wet wipes.) Wet wipes. That'd be my secret vice. I shoplift 'em like a bugger. I got to shower. You can close your eyes or feast your eyes. Up to you. *(She now proceeds to wipe in and around her clothes as she talks.)* I been raped nine times on the street, I wouldn't recommend it. *(Deals with a passerby.)* Spare change for my allergy medicine, sir? I only been raped once since I got the machete though. There's some gentlemen had to get a lotta stitches 'cause they couldn't keep it in their pants. I got a lot of skin diseases, they go with the territory. Spider bites, rat bites, bee stings, lot of non-specific infections. *(She stops washing and watches something go by.)* See those shoes? They run close to six hundred dollars. Oh, I got my own version of the antique road show. *(Writes in her notebook.)* Those shoes go into my study of the "too much." It runs about six thousand pages now.*(Puts away wet wipes.)* I got to serve dinner. *(Gets out a can of wet cat food and a can opener.)* I got silver. I got napkins. I got a candle for special occasions. My husband worked for Tyler Pipe, no safety precautions. He got crushed fixing a machine. C.E.O. got a hundred million dollar golden parachute. *(Makes a note. Opens cat food.)* I used to eat Nine Lives, but there's considerably more calcium in Purrfect Kitty. I wouldn't want to get the osteoporosis. *(Passerbys.)* Got three hundred dollars so I can cap a tooth, sir? Any spare chandeliers, ma'am. *(She eats.)* Car over there cost sixty thousand. Guy's watch cost fourteen hundred. Woman's nose job and botox, priceless. *(She chuckles. She eats.)* Cats aren't the beneficiaries of a whole helluva lot of flavor. Personally I like it with Jalapeflos when I can get 'em. You get interested in the "too much," it's pretty prevalent. Makeup on that lady, I'm gonna say forty dollars. Diamond-studded cat collar? I'm not gonna think about it. *(Finishes eating.)* Mmmm-mmmn-good. *(Tosses can.)* I liter like a bugger. Way I look at it you're either part of the "too much" or you're not. Some day there's a bunch of us are gonna get pissed off. *(Passerby.)* Trying to save up for an amputation, sir. *(Pulls out a toothbrush.)* Got to brush my teeth. Now toothpaste, that's part of the too much. I keep sand in my pocket. *(She dips toothbrush in a side pocket and then brushes.)* I don't like shelters. Us "too littles," we smell like hell. I go there I shove a clove up each nostril. I got a daughter somewhere, that much is true. Eleven years old now. I lost track of her. Okay, Amelie, she's ready to call it at day. *(Looks in her notebook.)* I made nine dollars thirty-two cents today. What'd you make? *(Watches something go by.)* Three hundred dollar skateboard. *(Gets out her machete.)* Don't fuck with me, I sleep light. *(Looks up.)* Last of the sun, must be 9:14. Saw in the paper today they're selling houses for way over a million dollars. *(Sits down.)* Let Amelie do this once more for you. *(Pours out coins.)* Billy takes fifty cents, Jimmy takes a quarter, Audrey takes twenty cents, how much does that leave for Donna, Posy and Amelie? *(She rolls over ready for sleep.)* Sleep tight.

ALEXANDER

ACTRESS. I had a boyfriend whose hobby was quiet. His full name was Alexander Shoeshine Walker. His father gave each of his six children middle names that described what he was doing at the hour of their birth. Alexander said it was a measure of his childhood that none of their middle names was delivery room. Alexander said he grew up with a lot of shouting, worked in a tool and dye factory, played for nine years in a heavy metal cover band and now he's addicted to silence. Alexander is very handsome and intelligent and caring and funny, but he will only talk to me one hour a night. And half hour in the morning, a half hour in the afternoon and one at night. He doesn't talk at all on Saturdays, but he'll talk all day Sunday though he's pretty cranky by nightfall: I love this man but I am giving our relationship some pretty serious thought. I'm a librarian, I mean he will only talk on his schedule. He does say my silence has

a very particular quality which is why he wants to be with me for-
ever. He finds my silence evocative and erotic. I've never said this
to anyone but it's his favorite form of foreplay. We sit perfectly still
and look directly into each other's eyes and then suddenly we grab
each other and do it like tigers. It's pretty amazing. Other than that I
have a problem. I'm one of those people who always did homework
with the T.V. on. I'm like a pretty compulsive talker. A silence that
extends for more than five minutes drives me quite literally insane.
I quite often think of killing Alexander, and I feel that may be a bad
thing for the relationship. On Saturdays which are completely de-
void of sound I eventually run into the woods and bite trees and eat
smalls rocks. Alexander says don't worry, that this is a transitional
period for my sound addiction but I don't think so. You know how
they used to personify Death in movies, novels and plays? What I
really think is that Alexander is Death and that he's come for me. I
know it's nutty but it's actually what I think. Tonight I'm taking the
bus to Chicago, which Consumer Reports says is like the noisiest
city in America. No matter what the sex is like, never let anyone
take away your voice.

OTHER FOLK'S SHOES

ACTRESS. I once rode with 23,000 bikers 'cross the middle of Mas-
sachusetts and there were six or seven of 'em weren't lawyers. How
you gonna get an outsider image goin' when all the insiders wanna
be outsiders without none of the risk and deprivations? My brother
One-Ball showed me this fashion magazine where these models was
tryin' to look like heroin addicts. They was pretendin' to be passed
out on the ground, lying on broken glass an' discarded works and all
like that, but I'm here to tell you their damn lipstick was perfect. I'd
call that the dark side of the grass is always greener. All that, that'd
make a pretty good national holiday, huh? Insiders go outside, out-

siders go inside. Work like this. Homeless folks shack up in the mansion, mansion folks camp under the bridge. Old folks go out and party, young folks stay in and watch golf. Black folks go to a white church, white folks go to a good church. You come up here do some acting, I sit out there unwrap little candies, fall asleep in the first row. You get the idea, right? Churches, they'd get behind it. Parents, they'd see the value for their kids. Teachers would call it a teachin' tool. I'm thinkin' August you know, 'cause I don't think there's a single good holiday in August. Get the whole thing set up nationwide easy as pie. But see, I'd fix it so there was a little twist, a little zinger to it. Mornin' after here comes the surprise. Have-nots don't give any of it back. See the have-nots would be the Government, the police, the military high command, the C.E.O's and they'd be sittin' in the three million dollar homes back of those gates with the alarms on and the dead locks locked. Then I'd go in the Dave Letterman Show dressed like Dave Letterman and I'd say, "guess what you damn fools, that wasn't no holiday that was the revolution! Done deal, not a drop of blood spilled, over and out." *(Walks toward audience.)* Lets have some fun. Change clothes with me. *(A pause.)* Just for a minute.

SCORE

ACTRESS. The only insolvable problem with life has been that there is no final score. They used to say that whoever dies with the most toys wins but by the time you die there are better toys. Problem now solved. Galactic Technologies allows you, finally, to live life to win and even possibly go to a bowl game. Released today, our new computer programs have created the International Competitive Living League, or the I.C.L.L. as you'll be reading in your sports page tomorrow. This, ladies and gentlemen, will finally allow you to make some real sense out of your existence. Are you, we ask, in the big time or are you living a bush league life? You can compete with your neighborhood, nation or internationally with others of your own sex, religion, economic group, food preferences, married state, occupation and automotive interests or you can cross-category. You will no longer wake up worrying where you stand, you will know exactly. The I.C.L.L. takes into account your fiscal well being, spiritual state, sexual abilities, number of friends, sense of the big picture, personal style, magazine subscriptions, work hours, charitable giving, prescription use, calorie count, number of people who actually know your name and the affectionate regard of your pets. High and low marks translate, you see, on a competitive scoring grid weekly, giving you a full season of life games, playoffs, bowl games, national rankings and, every four years, the Olympics. By next year Galactic Technologies will have a program where you can be drafted and turn pro. No more anxiety about whether you're a success or a failure; it's going to be down there for all of us to see in black and white. Secretly, we know you want to know. What's your score? It's going to be posted. You might as well compete.

THE LINE

ACTRESS. Excuse me, sir, but I believe you've just stepped in front of me in the line. It's a pretty long line and I've been standing here in it a pretty long time. Sir, the package I am waiting to mail weighs 37 pounds, and I don't have a whole lot of upper body arm strength. We live in a world where civilization as we know it teeters on a knife edge and, lest we decline into unmentionable chaos, we are reliant on courtesy. Excuse me? You told who to save your place in line while you dealt with your car alarm? Did he ask you, Madam? Well, if you didn't ask her, whom did you ask? Sir, if the person you asked to secure your place in line has subsequently left the line, your place is not secured. I should inform you that I am not considered by those who know me well to be a particularly stable personality. Historically I deal badly with stress and in ways unsuitable to most social situations. In a cry for help I ask you to step from out in front of me in this line. All right, as you are not amenable to reason, allow me to read you the warning on my label. Three years ago a certain Bertrand Samocri swerved into a parking place I had waited long and patiently for. I then followed Mr. Samocri home where I shot him with a tranquilizer dart obtained from my brother, a zookeeper, and then placed Mr. Samocri on a garbage scow sailing, I believe, for Central America. In his absence, I set fire to his garage and filled his pick-up truck with wet cement. Thank you, sir, I deeply appreciate your responsible decision to leave the line. Allow me to wish you all the best. Bye. *(A pause, she winks.)* Works every time.

THE STATE

ACTRESS. And if you don't mind, bring the salad with the entree, mustard vinaigrette on the side. Nice ring? Yes, thank you so much for noticing. Ruby circlet around the diamonds, that's right. You wonder about the value, don't you? I see you do. High six figures, does that help? We're disapproving, aren't we? Your little waitress economics probably equate this with a lifetime's wages for a million Americans or some such, yes? Oh dear. Allow me to say this to you, I am filthy rich and I am really, really sick of being criticized and satirized. I made it, it's mine and it's not my fault that I have 300 million and you don't. There's no reason you couldn't get in to pharmaceuticals. And I don't want you to leave this conversation thinking I hate the poor. I could, you know, there are many perfectly good reasons to hate the poor. They are disproportionately criminals, alcoholics and drug addicts, for one thing. The poor have dreadful taste and no aesthetics. They support strip malls. They litter. They produce no great novels, great paintings or great music. They...excuse

SEZ SHE

me, I'll go no further. I have no intention of hating the poor, and I have no intention of letting them ruin my life in the same way they have ruined public education. I am simply exhausted by being the object of their transferred self-loathing, which is precisely what I see in your eyes as you stare at my ring. So, dressing on the side, and please understand our little conversation as an explanation of why I'm tipping you 10%. I tip 20% for mastery and attitude, not for disdain, misplacement of the dessert spoon and tea spilled in the saucer. One moment. I had a thought as a generous amusement that, had I been well served, I might leave this ring as the gratuity. Noblesse oblige. But not today I fear. No, no, no, not today. Thank you so much. *(Pointing to the corner of her mouth.)* You have a crumb right here.

Also By

Jane Martin

ANTON IN SHOW BUSINESS

THE BOY WHO ATE THE MOON

CEMENTVILLE

CRIMINAL HEARTS

CUL DE SAC

FLAGS

FLAMING GUNS OF THE PURPLE SAGE

GOOD BOYS

JACK AND JILL

KEELY AND DU

MIDDLE AGED WHITE GUYS

MR BUNDY

SHASTA RULE

SOMEBODY/NOBODY

SUMMER

TALKING WITH...

TRAVELLIN' SHOW

VITAL SIGNS

SAMUELFRENCH.COM

OTHER TITLES AVAILABLE FROM SAMUEL FRENCH

VITAL SIGNS
Jane Martin

Monologues / 2m optional, 6f / Bare Stage
The author of *Talking With* and other hits has never been
funnier or more compelling than in this suite of theatrical
miniatures over thirty two minute monologues. The two men
in the cast are optional foils for the six compelling women
who perform a collage about contemporary woman in all
her warmth and majesty, her fear and frustration, her joy and
sadness. *Vital Signs* wowed audiences at the Humana Festival at
Actors Theatre of Louisville, where it was directed of Jon Jory
whose notes are published with the play.

"Vital and original."
– *The New York Times*

"Offers wonderful opportunities for actresses to show off their
versatility."
– *Washington Times*

OTHER TITLES AVAILABLE FROM SAMUEL FRENCH

TALKING WITH...
Jane Martin

Monologues / 11f / Bare Stage
These extraordinary monologues received a standing ovation
at Louisville's Actors Theatre. Idiosyncratic characters amuse,
move and frighten, always speaking from the depths of their
souls. They include a baton twirler, a fundamentalist snake
handler, an ex rodeo rider and an actress willing to go to any
length to get a job.

"A dramatist with an original voice ... [and] gladsome humor."
– *New York Times*

"With Jane Martin, the monologue has taken on a new poetic
form, intensive in its method and revelatory in its impact."
– *Philadelphia Inquirer*

**1982 winner of the American Theatre Critics Association
Award for Best Regional Play.**

SAMUELFRENCH.COM

CPSIA information can be obtained at www.ICGtesting.com
Printed in the USA
LVOW121438240212

270290LV00006B/6/P

9 780573 633430